The God Book

A Necessarily Incomplete Guide to the Essence of God

Featuring: My God Diary

Paul Yedwab

The God Book

A Necessarily Incomplete Guide to the Essence of God

Featuring: My God Diary

Paul Yedwab

UAHC Press
New York, New York

Typesetting: El Ot Ltd., Tel Aviv
This book is printed on acid-free paper.
Copyright © 2002 by **URJ Press**
Manufactured in the United States of America
10 9 8 7 6 5 4 3 2

For Ariella, Jesse, and Zoe

My ultimate proofs for the existence of a loving and gracious God

Contents

Contents

Acknowledgments

If Martin Buber is correct, we find God most profoundly in our relationships with others. That is most certainly true of me. My most spiritual moments have occurred standing not on some high mountain peak, but under the *chuppah* with my beautiful wife, Wendy, and again in the birthing room holding each of my children in my arms for the first time. So I thank my family with all my heart not only for allowing me the time to complete this book, but also for helping me to feel my subject, and for inspiring me in ways of holiness.

It is not easy growing up as the son of a rabbi and a Jewish educator, but my parents, Myra and Rabbi Stanley Yedwab, always allowed me, indeed encouraged me, to think for myself and even to rebel. Paradoxically, it was this very rebellion that first kindled my passion for the study of theology. We all do end up being like our parents, and I for one feel very lucky that this is so.

My colleagues at Temple Israel, Rabbis Harold Loss, Joshua Bennett, and Marla Hornsten, and Cantors Harold Orbach and Lori Corrsin have consistently encouraged me to teach what I love, and this freedom has led directly to the publication of this work.

My intense philosophical, and sometimes personal, discussions with Zohar Raviv were essential to putting Ezekielian flesh on the skeletons of my God curriculum. I thank him most humbly for his intellectual, academic, and spiritual generosity.

As I watched Rabbi Hara Person, my wonderful editor, shape my text as it developed, I could not help but think of a master sculptor working with very rough clay. I am deeply grateful to her, as I am to all who helped to make this dream come true. I would also like to thank those at the UAHC Press who helped give final shape to this book, including Ken Gesser, Stuart Benick, Rick Abrams, Liane Broido, Debra Hirsch Corman, and Sarah Gluck.

Introduction
Beyond Noah's Ark

Over the past two decades I have asked hundreds of teenagers from scores of temples and synagogues, youth movements and camps how they learned about God in their religious schools. Most of them point to Bible stories. When I ask which stories they remember studying most often, they generally single out the story of Noah. This is understandable. Kids love elephants and giraffes, rainbows are easy to paint, and the ark makes for great dioramas. Think for a moment, however, about the God concept that the story presents. It depicts a God who destroys most of the people of the earth because they are bad. If we were to evaluate our curricula strictly from a theological perspective, is this the story we would choose to emphasize? Is this the most representative, the most sophisticated, the most elevating, the most comforting, or even the most age-appropriate theological concept that we have to share? Of course not, but it is nonetheless the one our religious schools most frequently teach.

In my rabbinic thesis, "Naaseh V'nishma: Faith Development from a Jewish Perspective," I proposed that we build upon James Fowler's provocative suggestion that growth in faith is accelerated if the individual is introduced to faith stories that represent a level of faith beyond his or her own. This book is an attempt to do just that. In our modern age too many of our young people have thrown out God with the theological bath water. They have rejected the existence of a spiritual force in the universe simply because no one ever thought to discuss God with them in a more adult fashion. I view this book as a theological antidote—an antidote to premature atheism.

Many of the stories that you have come to expect in a book such as this will be missing. We are searching here for the nature of God, the essence, if you will. As a result, we will not be examining God's complete Jewish biography or historical resume. Hence the subtitle of this book: *A Necessarily Incomplete Guide to the Essence of God*.

Theology is the formal and systematic study of God ideas. This is not a theology textbook. It is, however, a thinking book, and a believing one. It is about ideas, about scientific reality, about the nature of the universe and of our lives. It is about God, and about the Jewish conceptions of God that are often ignored in our religious school classes. Although we will not make an exhaustive study of the major Jewish theologians and their writings, we will explore the questions that motivated them: How was the universe created? Do I have a soul? What happens to me after I die? Why do bad things happen to good people? Why should I be good? How can I access God? What is prayer and what should I pray for?

After each chapter, there is a section entitled "My God Diary." I urge you to use these pages to write about your feelings and thoughts, doubts and questions. I believe that you will find the process of writing a most revealing one. If writing does not appeal to you, use these questions as conversation starters at dinner or in class, around the game table or on the basketball court. You will also see that there are *italicized questions,* like the ones below, interspersed throughout the regular text. These are questions for discussion with your teachers or parents, classmates or friends, or for you to ponder on your own.

What are the questions that you have about God? What questions would you like this book to answer?

My God Diary
Entry #1

How did you learn about God as a child? Does your theological education match the one described in the Introduction? Which God stories do you remember?

1

2

Right now, as I begin this course of study, my understanding of God is that God is...

4

1. Our Father, Our King

Have you ever thought of God as an old man with a white beard, sitting up on a cloud, and holding some sort of staff or magic wand? If so, you are not alone. This is the first image that comes to many of us when we are asked to think about God.

The names and images we use for God have an effect on how we understand God. Consider, for instance, the blessing over the wine, a blessing many of us know well, and which is representative of so many other Jewish blessings and prayers.

בָּרוּךְ אַתָּה יְיָ, אֱלֹהֵינוּ מֶלֶךְ הָעוֹלָם, בּוֹרֵא פְּרִי הַגָּפֶן.

Baruch atah Adonai, Eloheinu Melech haolam, borei p'ri hagafen.

Blessed are You, *Adonai* our God, Sovereign (King) of the universe, Creator of the fruit of the vine.

In this blessing, God is represented in a variety of ways. What are they?

First, we refer to God with the second-person masculine singular pronoun אַתָּה, "You."

Do you generally think of God as a You, as an It, as a He, or as a She? Why? How might the pronoun we use to refer to God affect the ways in which we think about God?

Next, we refer to God, whom we call יְיָ אֱלֹהֵינוּ, *Adonai Eloheinu*, as מֶלֶךְ הָעוֹלָם, *Melech haolam*, "King of the universe."

5

Are there ways in which God is like a king? What are they? How is God different from a king?

As the T'filah, or Amidah prayer, begins, Jews traditionally take three steps forward and bow, as if entering the courtroom of a king. This is a powerful image for a royal subject. In our world, however, royalty is a distant concept. We no longer bow to kings or queens. To put it in more modern terms, think of yourself as entering God's living room for a heart-to-heart chat. In any case, when we pray the Amidah, it is as if we are entering God's presence.

Why do you think so many of the prayers in our siddur *refer to God as King? What does this tell us about the people who wrote the prayers?*

We conclude the prayer by calling God בּוֹרֵא, Borei, "Creator."

Can you point to any evidence that God created the world? What arguments could be made refuting this idea?

So we see that even in a simple blessing over wine we find several different images of the one and only God.

A classic science fiction story is entitled Flatland.[1] It depicts a two-dimensional world in which three-dimensional creatures suddenly land. How can these two-dimensional beings understand or even perceive these three-dimensional ones? We are in a similar predicament when we try to understand God. We are three-dimensional creatures striving to understand the nature of God, who is infinitely dimensional. That is our challenge.

My God Diary

Entry #2

As a child learning the prayers, did referring to God as "King" cause you to think of God as a man? If so, what do you think now?

What might it feel like to be in God's presence? Have you ever felt God's presence in your life? If so, when and how?

2. Like a Rock...

A major automobile company claims in its commercials that the trucks it makes are built "like a rock."

What are they trying to say about their pickups? How might a truck be "like a rock"?

No automobile, however, is really like a rock. If it were, it wouldn't go very fast. What are the attributes of a rock? A rock is strong and durable; it is also very slow. Imagine the advertisement: "Our trucks are like a rock; they travel from 0 to 60 in eight millennia." That company would go out of business quickly. To sell its trucks, this company is not being literal; rather, it is employing a simile. No simile or metaphor, however, is perfect.

Consider this God metaphor drawn from our *siddur:*

צוּר יִשְׂרָאֵל, קוּמָה בְּעֶזְרַת יִשְׂרָאֵל, וּפְדֵה כִנְאֻמֶךָ יְהוּדָה וְיִשְׂרָאֵל. גֹּאֲלֵנוּ, יְיָ צְבָאוֹת שְׁמוֹ, קְדוֹשׁ יִשְׂרָאֵל. בָּרוּךְ אַתָּה יְיָ, גָּאַל יִשְׂרָאֵל.

> O Rock of Israel, come to Israel's help. Our Redeemer is God Most High—the Holy One of Israel. We praise You, O God, Redeemer of Israel.

How might God be like a rock?

The prayer also refers to God as "Redeemer," which means "one who saves."

11

What might this tell us about the way in which the author of the prayer thought about God?

In this prayer God is also referred to as "the Holy One."

What does the word "holy" mean to you? What else is holy in your life?

Finally, we are told that God is "Most High."

Is God physically higher than we are? If so, how can God be "everywhere"? If God is not a physical being, where does God live?

In some ways, God is like a rock. God is thought to be strong and steadfast, permanent and timeless, dependable and eternal.

Most God metaphors carry within them a kernel of truth, but they also distort the reality of God. If we spoke of God only as a rock, for instance, Jewish children would grow up thinking of God as a mineral—Mount Rushmore, the Rock of Gibraltar, or a stone to skim on the surface of a quiet lake.

Similarly, God is like a king or queen. Just as a king or queen can be a powerful force in people's lives, God can be a powerful force in our lives. We do not believe, though, that God wears a robe and a crown, or carries a royal scepter.

It is important, therefore, to realize that God is beyond metaphors, beyond labels, beyond names. Through our study, we will find that God is so much more than "King," "Rock," an old man with a beard, or even . . . an elephant.

My God Diary

Entry #3

Do you see God as Redeemer in your own life? In the world at large? Why or why not?

Complete this sentence: In my opinion, God is like a

In what ways is your simile true? In what ways is it untrue?

3. A God By Any Other Name

There once were five blind men who came upon an elephant. The first one walked into something large and firm, and said, "My friends, an elephant is like a wall." The second man, however, had stumbled upon a different part of the elephant, and responded with a laugh, "What are you talking about, old man? An elephant is not like a wall; it is like a fire hose." The third man yelped in pain. "Ouch!" he cried, "an elephant is not like a hose at all; it is like a knife, and a very sharp one at that!" The fourth man shook his head. "Ah, but you all are wrong!" he exclaimed. "Clearly an elephant is only a skinny little piece of rope." Where-upon the fifth man piped in, "No, no, no! An elephant is like a tree trunk, and I think mine is moving!"

Based on a folktale

Like an elephant, God is greater than any of us individually can grasp or understand. Each of us has only a glimpse of the reality of the true God. But if we were to take all our images and combine them, we would come to a truer vision of the nature of God, who is one.

Throughout our history, Jews have used a myriad of metaphors, similes, labels, and names to describe the indescribable reality of God. None of these is complete; none is perfectly accurate.

Examine these traditional names for God.

What does each name tell you about the nature of God? What are the strengths and weakness of each? What do you think they might have signified to our ancestors?

17

הַמָּקוֹם, *HaMakom*—The Place

הַקָּדוֹשׁ בָּרוּךְ הוּא, *HaKadosh Baruch Hu*—the Holy One of Blessing

הַשֵּׁם, *HaShem*—The Name

אֵין סוֹף, *Ein Sof*—The Never-ending (the Infinite)

שְׁכִינָה, *Shechinah*—the Dwelling Presence (Note: *Shechinah* is a feminine noun.)

רִבּוֹנוֹ שֶׁל עוֹלָם, *Ribono Shel Olam*—the Master of the Universe

אָבִינוּ מַלְכֵּנוּ, *Avinu Malkeinu*—Our Sovereign Parent (literally, "our Father, our King")

אַב הָרַחֲמִים, *Av HaRachamim*—the Merciful Parent

אֱלֹהֵי אֲבוֹתֵינוּ, *Elohei Avoteinu*—the God of Our Ancestors

מָגֵן אַבְרָהָם וְעֶזְרַת שָׂרָה, *Magein Avraham v'Ezrat Sarah*—the Shield of Abraham and the Help of Sarah

שׁוֹמֵעַ תְּפִילָה, *Shomie-a T'filah*—the One Who Hears Our Prayers

אֵל יְשׁוּעָתִי, *El Yishuati*—God of My Redemption

אֵל עֶלְיוֹן, *El Elyon*—God on High

יְיָ רֹעִי, *Adonai Ro-i*—Adonai, My Shepherd

Which of the above names do you prefer? Why?
Do any of these names suggest new ideas of names for God to you?

God is God is God is God, but the names we use to refer to God affect what we think and feel about God.

My God Diary
Entry #4

If you had to create a new name for God, one that expresses an important characteristic of God, what would it be? What is the strong point of the name you have chosen? How is it an accurate depiction of יהוה? What are its weaknesses? How might it mislead us as to the nature of יהוה?

Why is it so common for us to think of God as a person, even though we know that, according to Jewish belief, God is not human?

4. *Ruach Elohim:* The Wind of God

Genesis 1:1–2

בְּרֵאשִׁית בָּרָא אֱלֹהִים אֵת הַשָּׁמַיִם וְאֵת הָאָרֶץ: וְהָאָרֶץ
הָיְתָה תֹהוּ וָבֹהוּ וְחֹשֶׁךְ עַל־פְּנֵי תְהוֹם וְרוּחַ אֱלֹהִים
מְרַחֶפֶת עַל־פְּנֵי הַמָּיִם.

In the beginning, God created the heavens and the earth,
and the earth was unformed and void, and darkness was on
the face of the deep, and רוּחַ אֱלֹהִים, *Ruach Elohim*, the Wind
of God, was hovering over the face of the water.

Literally, רוּחַ אֱלֹהִים, *Ruach Elohim,* means "the Wind of God."
Figuratively, it can also be understood as "the Spirit of God."

This metaphor is a profound one, for the Hebrew word for "soul" is
נְשָׁמָה, *n'shamah,* which means "a breath." In the Torah we are told
that we all are created בְּצֶלֶם אֱלֹהִים, *b'tzelem Elohim,* "in the image
of God." This does not mean that יהוה has brown hair, a chipped
tooth, or a freckled nose. Rather, it means that we have a breath of
יהוה within us, a נְשָׁמָה, *n'shamah.* If God is the spiritual "Wind of the
Universe," then each of us has a breath of that spirit within us—a
נְשָׁמָה, *n'shamah,* "a soul."

One way we can envision God, then, is as the "Spiritual Wind" that
animates our world and is also a part of each and every one of us.
Perhaps one of the best places to begin searching for God, therefore,
is within ourselves.

*If you wanted to find the breath of God within you, how would
you go about locating it?*

23

If we think of God as the Wind of Spirit that animates our universe, and if each of us has a breath of that Spiritual Wind within us, then what might happen to that breath of spirit when we die?

The Rabbis believed that we all have a soul and that the soul is eternal. They taught that when we die the soul returns to God in a spiritual place known as *Gan Eden*, the Garden of Eden. There the soul waits in God's presence for the Messianic Age to come, at which time all the souls will be revived in a perfect world of peace.

What do you think of this idea?

God is not the wind any more than God is a rock, but the metaphor stretches our understanding of the nature of God, who is, of course, also the God of nature.

My God Diary
Entry #5

What do you think happens to us after we die?

How could the idea of having a breath of God within you affect the choices you make in your life?

5. I Am What I Am

Moses has just been called by God to go and tell old Pharaoh to "let my people go." Moses is nervous and afraid. "Who am I," Moses asks in a quavering voice, "to go before Pharaoh and redeem the Israelites from Egypt?" (Exodus 3:11) God reassures Moses, saying, "I will be with you." But Moses still is concerned:

Exodus 3:13–14

וַיֹּאמֶר מֹשֶׁה אֶל־הָאֱלֹהִים הִנֵּה אָנֹכִי בָא אֶל־בְּנֵי יִשְׂרָאֵל
וְאָמַרְתִּי לָהֶם אֱלֹהֵי אֲבוֹתֵיכֶם שְׁלָחַנִי אֲלֵיכֶם וְאָמְרוּ־לִי
מַה־שְּׁמוֹ מָה אֹמַר אֲלֵהֶם: וַיֹּאמֶר אֱלֹהִים אֶל־מֹשֶׁה
אֶהְיֶה אֲשֶׁר אֶהְיֶה וַיֹּאמֶר כֹּה תֹאמַר לִבְנֵי יִשְׂרָאֵל אֶהְיֶה
שְׁלָחַנִי אֲלֵיכֶם.

So Moses said to God, "When I come to the Israelites and
say to them, 'The God of your fathers has sent me to you,'
and they ask me, 'What is this God's name?' what should
I tell them?" And God responded to Moses, *Ehiyeh Asher
Ehiyeh*, I Will Be What I Will Be."

I call this the "Doris Day theology" (because Doris Day once sang a famous song that went, "*Que sera sera*, whatever will be, will be"). Others translate this phrase as "I am what I am" (which I call the "Popeye theology"). However you translate it, it is a wonderful name for God. It helps us think of God as something other than a person.

The name "God" sounds a lot like a human name. Try saying, "God runs, God jumps," or even "God scores on the rebound." It works, doesn't it? But now try saying, "I Will Be What I Will Be runs." Somehow, it just doesn't sound right, and it shouldn't.

29

Can you think of other examples in which our language controls our thought?

Can you think of someone or something that is poorly named? Something or someone whose name seems to fit perfectly?

In the very next verse God confirms this choice of name and makes it permanent. God says,

זֶה־שְׁמִי לְעֹלָם וְזֶה זִכְרִי לְדֹר דֹר.

"This will be My name forever, and this is how I should be referred to for all time."

Names, however, have a way of being shortened. Even God gets a nickname, and *Ehiyeh Asher Ehiyeh* is shortened to יהוה *(yod-hei-vav-hei).*

No one knows how יהוה was pronounced by the Children of Israel. Tradition tells us that this sacred and secret name was uttered only once a year, on Yom Kippur, by the High Priest, and only in the Holy of Holies. Some scholars believe that it was pronounced *Yehovah.* Others suggest that it should be rendered as *Yahweh.* Think of the power of a God who is beyond names!

"I Will Be What I Will Be" is more than a name; it is a concept or an idea.

Is "I Am What I Am" exactly the same as "I Will Be What I Will Be," or do the two have slightly different meanings? What is the difference?

Today when we encounter the name יהוה we do not even try to say it as it was pronounced back then. Instead, we replace it with a substitute name, *Adonai,* which translates as "My Lord."

From this point forward, whenever you see the Hebrew word יהוה in the text, you can choose to replace it with the traditional rendering *Adonai* or the word "God," with "I Am What I Am" or "I Will Be What I Will Be," with one of the names we studied in chapter 3, or with any of the divine names that you create for yourself.

My God Diary
Entry #6

How does a God whose name you cannot even pronounce change your perceptions of God? Is this a God in whom it is easier or more difficult to believe?

How did you get your name? In what ways does it define you? Does your name adequately express who you are? What does your name say about you?

34

6. The Still Small Voice

In the Book of First Kings we find the story of Elijah the Prophet, who is locked in a battle with the priests of Baal, and with their patron, the evil queen Jezebel. After Jezebel threatens his life, Elijah goes into hiding. Tired, bedraggled, and despondent, he huddles in his cave.

I Kings 19:9–12

וַיָּבֹא־שָׁם אֶל־הַמְּעָרָה וַיָּלֶן שָׁם וְהִנֵּה דְבַר־יְהֹוָה אֵלָיו
וַיֹּאמֶר לוֹ מַה־לְּךָ פֹה אֵלִיָּהוּ: וַיֹּאמֶר קַנֹּא קִנֵּאתִי לַיהֹוָה
אֱלֹהֵי צְבָאוֹת כִּי־עָזְבוּ בְרִיתְךָ בְּנֵי יִשְׂרָאֵל אֶת־מִזְבְּחֹתֶיךָ
הָרָסוּ וְאֶת־נְבִיאֶיךָ הָרְגוּ בֶחָרֶב וָאִוָּתֵר אֲנִי לְבַדִּי וַיְבַקְשׁוּ
אֶת־נַפְשִׁי לְקַחְתָּהּ: וַיֹּאמֶר צֵא וְעָמַדְתָּ בָהָר לִפְנֵי יְהֹוָה
וְהִנֵּה יְהֹוָה עֹבֵר וְרוּחַ גְּדוֹלָה וְחָזָק מְפָרֵק הָרִים וּמְשַׁבֵּר
סְלָעִים לִפְנֵי יְהֹוָה לֹא בָרוּחַ יְהֹוָה וְאַחַר הָרוּחַ רַעַשׁ לֹא
בָרַעַשׁ יְהֹוָה: וְאַחַר הָרַעַשׁ אֵשׁ לֹא בָאֵשׁ יְהֹוָה וְאַחַר
הָאֵשׁ קוֹל דְּמָמָה דַקָּה.

And behold, the word of *Adonai* came to him saying, "What are you doing here, Elijah?" He responded, "I am zealous for *Adonai,* the God of Hosts, because the Israelites have abandoned Your covenant, destroyed Your altars, and murdered Your prophets with the sword. Only I have survived, and they are out to kill me." God said, "Go out and stand on this mountain before *Adonai.*"

And behold, *Adonai* passed by, and there blew a great and mighty wind, which split mountains and shattered boulders before *Adonai.* But *Adonai* was not in the wind. And after the wind there came thunder, but *Adonai* was not

in the thunder. And after the thunder, fire, but *Adonai* was
not in the fire. And after the fire came a still small voice.

So, according to the text, God was not in the wind or the thunder or
the fire, but rather in a still small voice. You have that still small voice
within you. Everyone does. This voice takes many forms. We may
hear it as the voice of comfort in times of sorrow, or as the voice that
urges us to stop and appreciate the beauty of nature. We might also
say that God is the voice of conscience—the still small voice that lets
us know the difference between right and wrong.

*Can you identify such a "still small voice" within yourself? What
form does it take?*

Once, when I was a young boy, I became infatuated with a group of
older boys at our campground, wanting desperately to be "one of the
gang." One day I came upon them playing, laughing, and cheering in
a circle. Grinning broadly, I ran up to be part of the group. Then I saw
the game they were playing. They had a penknife that they held over
a frog jumping around in the center of the circle. They were dropping
the knife repeatedly into the suffering animal, which was still hopping
frantically about, penned in by the laughing boys. I began to cry and
begged them to stop, but the leader of the group, who held the knife
between his fingers, just looked at me with a laugh and said, "You
don't understand. We're not trying to hit the frog. The goal of the
game is to miss the frog!" And with that, he dropped the knife
directly through the poor creature's eye. With a shrug he said, "Oops,
I lose."

I was only five, but I knew I had witnessed something evil. This was
not just something naughty, like teasing my sister, sneaking a cookie,
or even shoplifting from a store, but something much worse—the
deliberate infliction of pain on another living creature.

Have you ever witnessed, experienced, or become aware of an act that you instinctively knew was evil? What was it?

Because of the still small voice within us, however, we can also recognize goodness in our world. The spontaneous outpouring of generosity when the Twin Towers of the World Trade Center in New York were destroyed on September 11, 2001, and the courageous acts of heroism performed in the attack's aftermath by police officers, firefighters, and rescue workers were acts of goodness for which there is no earthly reward.

According to Charles Darwin's theory of the survival of the fittest, we human beings are simply animals, clawing and scraping and competing for survival and for the continuation of our gene pool. In many ways Darwin is probably correct. Even seemingly selfless acts may be construed as self-serving. You lend a hand to a friend, for instance, hoping to be invited over to swim in her pool. But what if there are some acts of goodness that bring no benefits? What if human beings have a soul that allows them to go ethically beyond what is in their own best interests? These are acts of altruism.

Consider, for example, the true story of the four chaplains in World War II. Four chaplains—Rabbi Alexander Goode, Father John Washington, the Reverend Clark Poling, and the Reverend George Fox—were serving on the USS *Dorchester* when it was torpedoed by a German U-boat one hundred miles off the coast of Greenland. The ship almost immediately began to sink into the freezing waters of the sea. Unfortunately, there were not enough life preservers on board. Seeing this, the four chaplains, who were officers and were already suited in their life vests, removed them and handed them to four seamen, who otherwise would have drowned. The ship sank eighteen minutes after it was hit. Witnesses describe the four chaplains standing arm-in-arm and singing psalms together as the ill-fated ship went down into the icy waters.

And what about *tzedakah*? Certainly, some charitable acts can be explained as self-serving. By giving to charity a person might improve his or her standing in the community, for instance. On the other hand, each of us can point to so many acts of generosity that have no inherent benefit for the donor: the donation of blood marrow or a kidney for an unknown patient hundreds of miles away, or charitable contributions that are given anonymously. How can these be explained by the theory of survival of the fittest?

If we were merely animals grubbing for survival, what would make a human being commit an altruistic act? Perhaps there is a still small voice within us that helps us to recognize the difference between good and evil, and allows us to act in ways of righteousness, charity, and altruism.

My God Diary
Entry #7

Do you think altruism is possible? Have you ever witnessed, experienced, or become aware of an act of altruism? What was it?

40

In your opinion, what causes evil in the world?

7. The Sounds of Silence

The great biblical commentator Rashi has a different translation of the phrase קוֹל דְּמָמָה דַקָּה, kol d'mamah dakah, which was translated in the previous chapter as a "still small voice." Rashi translates the words literally. קוֹל, kol, means "voice" or "sound." דְּמָמָה, d'mamah, means "silence," and דַקָּה, dakah, means "soft." So the phrase can be translated as the "soft voice of silence," or even as the "sounds of silence."

In other words, God may have spoken to Elijah in something even softer than a whisper. Indeed, the communication may have been entirely nonverbal—a silent moment of transcendence, of understanding, of truth.

Which brings us to the question: What language does יהוה speak? Did God speak to Abraham and Moses and the prophets in Hebrew, or in some special divine language? Did God dictate the Torah to Moses, word for word, or was Moses translating God's divine thoughts?

According to Jewish tradition, the whole Torah was given at Sinai, along with the Oral Law, which later was written down as the Talmud. If you read the story of the giving of the Torah in the Torah text itself, however, it appears that only the Ten Commandments were given to Moses.

Exodus 20:1–3

וַיְדַבֵּר אֱלֹהִים אֵת כָּל־הַדְּבָרִים הָאֵלֶּה לֵאמֹר: אָנֹכִי יְהֹוָה
אֱלֹהֶיךָ אֲשֶׁר הוֹצֵאתִיךָ מֵאֶרֶץ מִצְרַיִם מִבֵּית עֲבָדִים:
לֹא־יִהְיֶה לְךָ אֱלֹהִים אֲחֵרִים עַל־פָּנָי.

God spoke all of these words, saying: I am *Adonai*, your God who brought you out of the land of Egypt, the house of bondage: You shall have no other gods before Me....

What follows is the rest of the Ten Commandments, not the entire Torah from beginning to end, as Jewish tradition teaches. To make matters even more complicated, this story of the Revelation at Sinai is retold in the Book of Deuteronomy. It seems that God again speaks only the Ten Commandments rather than the whole Torah at Sinai, but in this version, after the Ten Commandments are listed, there is an addendum:

Deuteronomy 5:19

אֶת־הַדְּבָרִים הָאֵלֶּה דִּבֶּר יְהוָה אֶל־כָּל־קְהַלְכֶם בָּהָר מִתּוֹךְ הָאֵשׁ הֶעָנָן וְהָעֲרָפֶל קוֹל גָּדוֹל וְלֹא יָסָף וַיִּכְתְּבֵם עַל־שְׁנֵי לֻחֹת אֲבָנִים וַיִּתְּנֵם אֵלָי.

Adonai spoke these words, **and no more**, to your whole congregation at the mountain, out of the fire and the thick cloud, in a mighty voice, and *Adonai* inscribed them on two stone tablets, which *Adonai* then gave to me.

The phrase "and no more" supports the interpretation that only the Ten Commandments were given at Sinai, an idea that is contrary to the tradition. In cases such as this, midrash comes to the rescue. In *Sh'mot Rabbah*, for instance, Rabbi Simeon ben Lakish, also known as Reish Lakish, explains the phrase "and no more" this way:

Sh'mot Rabbah 29:9

מהו ולא יסף אלא כשאדם קורא לחבירו יש לקולו בת קול והקול שהיה יוצא מפי הקב״ה לא היה לקולו בת קול.

45

What is the meaning of "and no more"? When a man calls his friend, there is an echo to his voice, but when God spoke there was no echo.

In other words, the phrase "and no more" refers only to the tenor of God's voice rather than to the content of the revelation.

In his mystical commentary on the Torah, *Zera Kodesh* (Seed of Holiness), Rabbi Naftali Tzvi Horowitz of Ropshitz (1760–1827), also known as the Ropshitzer Rebbe, points to another possible solution.

Zera Kodesh: On the Festival of Shavuot

נ״ל ע״ד ששמעתי מֶן פי אדמו״ר מרימנאב מהר״ם ז״ל
ע״פ אחת דיבר אלקים כו׳ שאפשר שלא שמענו מפי
הקב״ה רק אות א׳ דאנכי.

I believe, based on the teachings of my master, my mentor, and my teacher, Rabbi Menachem Mendel of Rymanov, may his memory be a blessing, who based himself on the biblical verse, GOD HAS SPOKEN ONCE; TWICE HAVE I HEARD; THAT POWER BELONGS TO GOD (Psalm 62:12) that it is possible that we did not hear from the mouth of the Holy One of Blessing, anything but the letter *alef* of the word *Anochi* (which is the first letter of the first word of the Ten Commandments).

Of course, the א, *alef,* is silent! In other words, there was a silent moment of spiritual knowing, and from that great pregnant silence, the Torah was created. What a remarkable idea!

Which explanation of "and no more" do you prefer? That of Reish Lakish or that of the Ropshitzer Rebbe and his teacher, Rabbi Menachem Mendel of Rymanov? Why? What are the implications of each for the nature of Torah? For the nature of divine communication?

The Ropshitzer Rebbe goes on to explain:

כי ידוע שכתבו ספרי מוסר ששם הוי' נרמז באות א'
שהוא צורת ב' יודי"ן וא"ו באמצע.

It is known by those who wrote the books of our tradition that the sacred name יהוה is hinted at by the letter *alef*, since an *alef* is formed by two *yods* and a *vav* in the middle.

If the Israelites heard the sound of the *alef*, and the *alef* is a representation of the essence of יהוה, then the Children of Israel experienced God directly at Sinai, not through words, but through an even more direct mode of understanding.

Is it indeed possible to communicate without words? How so?

What implications does this midrash have for the nature of Revelation, of Judaism, of relationships between God and human beings?

The Ropshitzer Rebbe, however, does not stop there. He takes his theory one amazing step further.

ושכן נרמז בפני האדם ב' עינים דוגמת צורת ב' יודי"ן
והחוטם דוגמת אות וא"ו והוא דוגמת אל"ף.

In addition, this form is hinted at in the face of every human being. The two eyes being examples of the form of two *yods*, and the nose corresponding to the letter *vav* so that the whole face is a manifestation of the letter *alef.*

 וע״ז כתיב בצלם אלקים עשה את האדם כי בצלם אדם חקוק צורת אות א׳ שמורה שם הוי׳ כנ״ל.

And this is why it is written GOD CREATED HUMAN BEINGS IN THE IMAGE OF GOD (Genesis 1:27). Because in the form of human beings is engraved the form of the letter *alef,* which guides us to the sacred name, יהוה, as mentioned above.

What are the implications of having the image of יהוה inscribed in our very faces?

Let us see what the Ropshitzer Rebbe has to say.

והנה ידוע שצלם הוא האור המקיף נגד צורה של אדם ונחנו עם קדוש מוזהרים ע״ז לצייר תמיד נוכחינו צלם זה לידע שחותם ה׳ נגד פניו ולדמות צורה ליוצרה וזהו אמרם ז״ל כלל גדול בתורה שכאשר זכינו למעמד הנבחר ושמענו קול יוצא האות אל״ף אז נכלל ונתגלה לנו צורת האות א׳ כמ״ש וכל העם רואים את הנשמע ראינו צורת הא׳ שמורה על שם הוי׳ וראו והבינו שזה ג״כ צורת פניהם וז״ש למען תהי׳ יראתו על פניכם לבלתי תחטאו כי כשאדם הולך תמיד במחשבה זו לא במהרה הוא חוטא.

And, behold, it is known that this image is the orbiting light around the form of every human being. And we as a holy people are admonished about this, to create always in front of us this image in order to know that the impression of God is before us always, and to equate our own image with the Creator. And this is what our ancestors, of blessed memory, established as a basic principle in the Torah, that when we merited to stand at Sinai and to hear the sound of the *alef*, then we realized and it was revealed to us the form of the letter *alef*, which guides us to the holy name יהוה. And we saw and we understood that this was also the form of our own faces, as it is said, AND MOSES SAID TO THE PEOPLE, FEAR NOT, FOR GOD HAS COME TO TEST YOU, TO SEE THAT THE FEAR OF GOD IS IN YOUR FACES, SO THAT YOU WILL NOT GO ASTRAY (Exodus 20:17) because a human being who walks always with this thought will not be quick to sin.

In the *V'ahavta* prayer we are admonished to keep God's commandments "as frontlets before our eyes." Here we are asked to remember that our eyes themselves are part of the letter *alef*, symbol of the presence of יהוה within us.

Sometimes, it would seem, God's divine voice can be heard in the sounds of silence.

My God Diary
Entry #8

What language does God speak: English, Hebrew, or God's own language? How do you think Moses came to hear God's thoughts? Through his ears? In his mind? Through some other form of Revelation?

Is it true that one who walks always with the understanding that we are made in the image of God will be
slower to sin? Why? Is יהוה the source of ethical
behavior?

8. You've Got a Friend: Buber's I—Eternal Thou

Do you have a friend? Not a buddy to hang out with, or a companion to keep you company, but a true friend—someone with whom you have shared profound moments of mutual understanding and appreciation? According to the great twentieth-century existentialist Jewish philosopher Martin Buber, those special moments of "knowing" constitute what he calls an I-Thou relationship. Generally we relate to others in the I-It mode. We use them to fulfill our own goals or objectives. This is appropriate and necessary. The mail carrier brings the mail and we take our letters, say thank you, and go about our business. We ask a dinner companion to pass the butter. There is nothing negative about this; it is simply a necessary part of living in the world. Even with those we love, an I-Thou moment cannot last forever. If it did, we would never be able to go to work or school, or get anything done. In fact, once we are aware that we have had an I-Thou moment, it is by definition over, for we are already putting labels on the experience.

I and Thou, First Part; page 59

When I experience another person as a Thou, and have an I-Thou experience with him/her, then s/he is not a thing among things, nor does s/he consist of material qualities. S/he is no longer merely a pronoun (a He or a She), limited by other He's and She's, a dot in the universal grid of time and space. Nor is s/he a characteristic that can be experienced and then described. S/he is not merely a loose bundle of labeled qualities. Standing alone and whole, s/he is Thou, and fills my universe. It is not as if there were nothing but s/he. Rather, it is as if everything else lives in his/her light.

This is true in the same way as a song is not merely a collection of tones, nor a verse a mere collection of words, nor a statue a collection of lines. One must tear and break apart in order to make a unified whole revert back to its component parts. So it is with the person whom I call Thou. I can abstract from him/her the color of his/her hair or the shadings of his/her speech, or the aura of his/her graciousness, and in fact I must often do this, but as soon as I do, s/he is no longer Thou.

Adapted from Martin Buber, *I and Thou*, trans. Walter Kaufmann
(Edinburgh: T & T Clark, 1970)

An I-Thou relationship is also mutual; it is a relationship between equals. It cannot be exploitative in any way. It is a moment of true "knowing" and understanding, and it is our ability to have such moments with another, a "Thou," that makes us fully, wholly, and joyfully human.

I and Thou, First Part; page 62

The Thou encounters the I by grace; it cannot be found by seeking.... The basic I-Thou must be experienced with one's whole being... can never be accomplished without me. I require a Thou to become I. Being I, I encounter Thou. All life is encounter.

What does Buber mean when he says, "All life is encounter?" Do you agree? Is there any part of your life that is not lived in relationship to others?

If you cannot force an I-Thou moment to happen, are there ways to make it more likely to occur?

According to Buber, it is within such relationships that we find God, or "live in the spirit."

> *I and Thou,* Second Part; page 89
>
> Spirit is not in the I, but between an I and a Thou. It is not like the blood that circulates in you, but like the air in which you breathe. A human being lives in the spirit when s/he is able to respond to his/her Thou. S/he is able to do that when s/he enters into this relationship with his/her whole being. It is solely by virtue of this power to relate that we are able to live in the spirit.

What do you think of Buber's idea that we can find God, or "live in the spirit," through our relationships to others?

The "Eternal Thou" is Buber's term for God.

> *I and Thou,* Third Part; page 123
>
> Extended, the lines of relationships intersect in the Eternal Thou. Every single Thou is a glimpse of that. Through every single Thou we address the Eternal Thou.

What does Buber mean when he says that we address the Eternal Thou through every single Thou?

Buber's relationship with God, the Eternal Thou, however, is not confined to I-Thou relationship moments with other people. Buber is an existentialist. That means that he argues out of his own experience, his own existence. From his own experience then, he shares with us a very specific I-Thou relationship that he has had. It is a relationship with an Eternal Thou, a tangible presence in his life, whom we call יהוה.

I and Thou, Third Part; page 127

Of course, God is the wholly other; but God is also the wholly same; the wholly present. God is certainly the tremendous mystery that appears and overwhelms. But God is also the mystery of the obvious that is closer to me than my own I.

However, even I–Eternal Thou relationships cannot last forever. Inevitably, they lose their spontaneity and slip into the realm of I-It.

I and Thou, Third Part; page 123

Human beings have addressed their Eternal Thou by many names. When they sang of what they had thus named, they still meant Thou; the first myths were hymns of praise. Then the names entered into the It-language; people felt impelled more and more to think of, and to talk about, their Eternal Thou as an It. But all the names of God remain sacred because they have been used not only to speak of God, but to speak to God as well.

Evaluate Buber's theory of the I-Thou in terms of your own experience. Does it ring true? What about his theory of the I–Eternal Thou?

In the section of the prayer service known as "The *Sh'ma* and Its Blessings," we find a prayer for creation, a prayer for revelation, and a prayer for redemption. While the other prayers are named appropriately, the revelation prayer is known as the אַהֲבָה, *Ahavah*,

57

or the "prayer of love." In other words, it is by revealing ourselves to others that we truly show them our love. Similarly, God's revelation to Abraham and Sarah was an act of *ahavah,* or love—an I–Eternal Thou moment.

Martin Buber cannot prove to you that such an Eternal Thou exists. He is not a rationalist who would try to demonstrate that his argument is correct with a system of logical proofs. Instead, he simply describes his experience of the world to you. If you have had such moments, he believes that you will understand.

Do you?

My God Diary
Entry #9

Have you experienced an I-Thou moment with another person? If so, describe it.

Have you ever experienced such a moment with a
transcendent other, an Eternal Thou? If so, describe the
moment.

9. A Stairway to Heaven

According to Martin Buber, once we know that we are having an I–Eternal Thou moment, it is over. In the Book of Genesis, our forefather Jacob has a similar experience.

Jacob has just stolen the birthright of his brother, Esau. As a result, he has fled for his life. Now he is scared and alone.

Genesis 28:10–15

וַיֵּצֵא יַעֲקֹב מִבְּאֵר שָׁבַע וַיֵּלֶךְ חָרָנָה: וַיִּפְגַּע בַּמָּקוֹם וַיָּלֶן שָׁם כִּי־בָא הַשֶּׁמֶשׁ וַיִּקַּח מֵאַבְנֵי הַמָּקוֹם וַיָּשֶׂם מְרַאֲשֹׁתָיו וַיִּשְׁכַּב בַּמָּקוֹם הַהוּא: וַיַּחֲלֹם וְהִנֵּה סֻלָּם מֻצָּב אַרְצָה וְרֹאשׁוֹ מַגִּיעַ הַשָּׁמָיְמָה וְהִנֵּה מַלְאֲכֵי אֱלֹהִים עֹלִים וְיֹרְדִים בּוֹ: וְהִנֵּה יְהוָה נִצָּב עָלָיו וַיֹּאמַר אֲנִי יְהוָה אֱלֹהֵי אַבְרָהָם אָבִיךָ וֵאלֹהֵי יִצְחָק הָאָרֶץ אֲשֶׁר אַתָּה שֹׁכֵב עָלֶיהָ לְךָ אֶתְּנֶנָּה וּלְזַרְעֶךָ: וְהָיָה זַרְעֲךָ כַּעֲפַר הָאָרֶץ וּפָרַצְתָּ יָמָּה וָקֵדְמָה וְצָפֹנָה וָנֶגְבָּה וְנִבְרְכוּ בְךָ כָּל־מִשְׁפְּחֹת הָאֲדָמָה וּבְזַרְעֶךָ: וְהִנֵּה אָנֹכִי עִמָּךְ וּשְׁמַרְתִּיךָ בְּכֹל אֲשֶׁר־תֵּלֵךְ וַהֲשִׁבֹתִיךָ אֶל־הָאֲדָמָה הַזֹּאת כִּי לֹא אֶעֱזָבְךָ עַד אֲשֶׁר אִם־עָשִׂיתִי אֵת אֲשֶׁר־דִּבַּרְתִּי לָךְ.

Jacob left Beer-sheba and set out for Haran. He came upon a certain place and stopped there for the night, for the sun had set. Taking one of the stones of that place, he put it under his head and lay down in that place. He had a dream. And behold, a stairway was set on the ground and its top reached to the heavens. And angels of God were going up and down on it. And behold, *Adonai* was standing on top of it and said, "I am *Adonai*, the God of your father

Abraham and the God of Isaac. The ground on which you lie, I will give to you and to your descendants. Your descendants shall be as the dust on the earth, and will spread westward and eastward, to the north and to the south. All the families of the earth shall bless themselves through you and your offspring. Remember, I am with you. I will protect you wherever you go and will bring you back to this land. I will not leave you until I have done what I have told you."

יהוה. appears just when Jacob needs support and help. And יהוה responds with reassurance and comfort. יהוה tells Jacob that the Land of Israel will belong to his descendants, that they will prosper, and that others will bless themselves through them. Finally, יהוה reassures Jacob that he will not be alone, that יהוה will always be with him. What could be more comforting?

In your opinion, does יהוה's promise of the Land of Israel have an impact on the modern political struggle in the Middle East? Why or why not?

That Jacob sees יהוה as being at the top of a stairway or ladder is intriguing. The image of a tunnel through which the soul can travel up to the presence of the Divine is found in many mystical traditions. In the Kabbalah, this process of spiritual elevation is known as "going up to the *Pardes* [garden]." In our text, Jacob sees God standing at the top of a stairway (or tunnel?), upon which angels (or souls?) are ascending and descending.

The mystics of the Kabbalah speak of "going up to the Pardes *[garden]." Does this mean that God lives in a place with trees and flowers? If not, what image are they trying to express?*

Jacob has had an I–Eternal Thou moment, an extraordinary moment of Revelation. But, as with every I-Thou moment, he does not recognize that it is happening until it is over.

Genesis 28:16

וַיִּיקַץ יַעֲקֹב מִשְּׁנָתוֹ וַיֹּאמֶר אָכֵן יֵשׁ יְהֹוָה בַּמָּקוֹם הַזֶּה
וְאָנֹכִי לֹא יָדָעְתִּי.

Jacob awoke from his sleep and said, "Surely, *Adonai* is in this place and I did not know it."

What does this line mean to you? How could Jacob not have known that God was there?

When we are in distress and in need of support, יהוה can come to us, but often it is not until later that we are able to stop and say, "Surely, God was in this place and I did not know it!"

My God Diary
Entry #10

Have you ever felt lost and alone? To whom did you turn for comfort? Was s/he able to help? Why or why not?

Have you ever had a dream that was important to you—a dream from which you awoke with a new perspective or sense of direction? What was it? How did it affect you?

10. Pow! The Mystical God of the Big Bang

Creation Theory #1:

In the beginning God had a problem. יהוה was everywhere, the universe was filled with the Divine Presence, so where was יהוה to put the world? So the *Ein Sof*, or Eternal God, contracted into *keilim*, or vessels. This process of contraction is called *tzimtzum*. Of course the vessels were finite and the *Ein Sof* infinite, so eventually the vessels exploded, and from that great explosion the universe was created.

Creation Theory #2:

In the beginning there was energy. At one point the energy began to contract and become increasingly dense. As a result of this contraction there was a great explosion, a Big Bang, from which the universe was created.

Theory #1 for the creation of the world comes to us from the Kabbalah, or Jewish mysticism. This idea was taught by the great Jewish mystic Isaac Luria, who lived more than five hundred years ago with his disciples in the city of Tzfat, in northern Israel. He came to this revelation through mystical means. He meditated on the meaning of Genesis, thus elevating his soul to commune with God.

Theory #2, often called the Big Bang theory, comes to us from the world of physics. In 1946, George Gamow, a Russian-born scientist, proposed that the "Big Bang," an intense concentration of pure energy, was the source of everything that exists in the universe.

According to this theory, the entire physical universe, including the four dimensions of time and space, burst forth from a state of infinite or near infinite density, temperature, and pressure.

Then, in 1965, two radio astronomers at the Bell Telephone laboratories in New Jersey, Arno Penzias and Robert Wilson, aimed their new reflector antenna at the heavens and picked up what they first thought was a background hiss caused by a malfunction in the antenna. They dismantled, cleaned, and put the antenna back together, but the strange sound persisted. It was not long before they realized that what they were hearing was an echo of the Big Bang. Subsequent data confirmed their findings and convinced most scientists that the world indeed was created from a Big Bang some fifteen billion years ago.

A Jewish mystic living in Tzfat more than five hundred years ago, and a Russian physicist of the twentieth century—how could they have come to such similar conclusions? After all, creation out of explosion is not exactly an obvious idea. Indeed, it is counterintuitive. Explosions destroy; they do not create! How did these two figures, distant from one another in so many ways, come to the same understanding? Perhaps because the theory simply is true. The two men came to understand a single truth, albeit through very different means.

Do you think there is such a thing as a single truth?

We often think of religion as standing in opposition to science. This, however, may not be the case. Consider these quotations from a well-known scientist of the twentieth century.

Can you guess who said them?

I want to know how God created this world. I am not interested in this or that phenomenon, in the specter of this or that element. I want to know His thoughts; the rest are details.[2]

My religion consists of a humble admiration of the illimitable superior spirit who reveals Himself in the slight details we are able to perceive with our frail and feeble minds. That deeply emotional conviction of the presence of a superior reasoning power, which is revealed in the incomprehensible universe, forms my idea of God.[3]

To the sphere of religion belongs the faith that the regulations valid for the world of existence are rational, that it is comprehensible to reason. I cannot conceive of a genuine scientist without that profound faith. The situation may be expressed by an image: science without religion is lame, religion without science is blind.[4]

It is only to the individual that a soul is given.[5]

Were you able to guess the source of the above quotations? See the next page for the answers.

They were all said by Albert Einstein, the most brilliant and intuitive physicist of the twentieth century. Einstein understood better than anyone that the universe is governed by certain physical laws. Underlying that order, however, Einstein perceived a master plan, and the author of that plan he called "God."

Thus we learn that it is entirely possible to be a religious rationalist, or a believing scientist!

My God Diary
Entry #11

Can the story of creation depicted in the Torah be true,
even if it is not scientifically accurate in every detail? Why
or why not?

In your opinion, how was the world created? What role did יהוה have in the creation of the world?

11. Maimonides and the God of Truth

Moses Maimonides, also known as the Rambam, lived in Egypt in the twelfth century C.E. He was said to be the greatest rabbi since the biblical Moses, who is often called our first rabbi. He was a physician, a rabbi, a philosopher, and a man of reason, and his writings reflect his profound intellect and breadth of knowledge. Maimonides laid out his theology in a remarkable work entitled *A Guide for the Perplexed*, published in Arabic in 1190 C.E. In the *Guide*, he sought to prove the existence of God according to rational principles. In this, he followed the great Greek philosopher Aristotle, whose works he had studied. Like Aristotle, Maimonides argued that the world must have had a Prime Mover, an original cause. Everything has a cause, he argued. Thus, if you go back far enough, logic dictates that there must have been a first cause, and this first cause, of course, was יהוה.

> *A Guide for the Perplexed* II:1
>
> It is as if you say: this stone, which was in motion, was moved by a staff; the staff was moved by a hand; the hand by tendons; the tendons by muscles; the muscles by nerves; the nerves by natural heat; and the natural heat by the form that subsists therein, this form being undoubtedly the Prime Mover.

Maimonides posits one rational proof of יהוה's existence. Can you propose any others?

If יהוה is indeed the Prime Mover, what has God been doing since then?

So יהוה, in the Rambam's mind, was a very real and powerful force in the universe. The Rambam, however, was insistent that יהוה was entirely incorporeal, that is to say, that יהוה has no body or physical attributes, despite the fact that we often speak of יהוה as having eyes, hands, or even a mind.

A Guide for the Perplexed I:46

There is a great difference between bringing to view the existence of a thing and demonstrating its true essence. We can lead others to notice the existence of an object by pointing to its characteristics, actions, or even most remote relations to other objects. In other words, if you wish to describe the king of a country to one of his subjects who does not know him, you can give a description and an account of his existence in many ways. You will either say to him, the tall man with a fair complexion and gray hair is the king, thus describing him by his characteristics; or you will say, the king is the person round whom are seen a great multitude of men on horse and on foot... or it is the person who ordered the building of that wall or the construction of that bridge...

What is Maimonides saying here about how we refer to others? Using words, try describing your best friend, or one of your parents. How close can you get to a true description?

Just as it is difficult to capture the essence of a person using "the language of children and men," so it is when we are referring to the infinite God.

A Guide for the Perplexed I:46

The same is the case with the information concerning the Creator given to the ordinary classes of men in all prophetic books and in the Torah. For it was found necessary to teach all of them that God exists, and that God is in every respect the most perfect Being....

That God exists was therefore shown to ordinary men by means of similes taken from physical bodies; that God is living by a simile taken from motion, because ordinary men consider only the body as fully, truly and undoubtedly existing....

In other words, in speaking of the infinite יהוה, human beings are constrained by finite language: nouns, verbs, adjectives, and adverbs. These are inadequate, but they are all we have.

A Guide for the Perplexed I:46

The perception by the senses, especially by hearing and seeing, is best known to us; we have no idea or notion of any other mode of communication between the soul of one person and that of another than by means of speaking, i.e., by the sound produced by lips, tongue and the other organs of speech. When, therefore, we are to be informed that God has a knowledge of things, and that communication is made by God to the Prophets who convey it to us, they represent God to us as seeing and hearing, i.e., as perceiving and knowing those things which can be seen and heard. They represent God to us as speaking, i.e., that communications from God reach the prophets....

Again, since we perform all these actions only by means of corporeal organs, we figuratively ascribe to God the organs of locomotion, as feet and their soles, organs of hearing, seeing and smelling as ear, eye and nose; organs and substance of speech as mouth, tongue and sound....

So far, what Maimonides is saying in his *Guide for the Perplexed* should not be too surprising. God does not really have hands; that is just our imperfect way of saying that God "does" something. Maimonides takes this concept one step further, applying it to God's "existence," to God's "life, power, wisdom, and will."

A Guide for the Perplexed I:56

Thus those who believe in the presence of essential attributes in God, such as Existence, Life, Power, Wisdom and Will, should know that these attributes, when applied to God, have not the same meaning as when applied to us....

Having made his case for the incorporeality of יהוה, Maimonides implores us to pass this understanding on to our children, lest they take these similes literally and thus misunderstand the true nature of יהוה.

A Guide for the Perplexed I:35

In the same way as all people must be informed, and even children must be trained in the belief that God is One, and that none besides God is to be worshiped, so must all be taught by simple authority that God is incorporeal; that there is no similarity in any way whatsoever between God and God's creatures; that God's existence is not like the existence of God's creatures, God's life not like that of any living being, God's wisdom not like the wisdom of the wisest of people; and that the difference between God and

God's creatures is not merely quantitative, but absolute as between two individuals of two entirely different types.

All this leaves us in a bit of a quandary. If it is true, as Maimonides says, that "anything predicated of God is totally different from our attributes and no definition can comprehend both," how then do we speak of God?

The Rambam has an answer for this as well. We cannot speak authoritatively of any attributes that God possesses. What we can identify, however, are those attributes that God does not possess. We may not be able to comprehend completely what God is, but we can know what God is not. Thus the "negative attributes of God" are available to us.

A Guide for the Perplexed I:58

Know that the negative attributes of God are the true attributes. They do not include any incorrect notions or any deficiency whatever in reference to God, while positive attributes imply polytheism and are inadequate.

In your opinion, what might be the negative attributes of יהוה*? What do we know that* יהוה *is not?*

Imagine! A God beyond names, a God beyond description, a God even beyond attributes. We have come a long way from the idea of God as an old man with a beard sitting on a cloud, watching over us with a magic wand!

My God Diary
Entry #12

How do you feel about a God that cannot be seen, heard, or even described, except by "negative attributes"? Why?

Why might this image of יהוה be difficult for some to embrace? How might it help others to believe in יהוה?

12. Our Mother, Our Chariot

The kabbalists of the sixteenth century believed that the *Ein Sof*, or Eternal God, was organized into *s'firot*, or spheres. The central, most essential sphere they refer to as the *Keter*, or Crown. The outermost sphere is known as the שְׁכִינָה, *Shechinah*, which is a feminine noun meaning "dwelling." The *Shechinah* is the aspect of the *Ein Sof* that human beings can access, that is with us always; it is the hovering, mothering presence of יהוה.

Why do you suppose that the kabbalists chose a feminine noun to describe the aspect of God to whom we as human beings can relate?

In ancient Israel, the people believed that יהוה dwelt with them in the Holy Temple of Jerusalem.

Are there certain places where יהוה lives? Are there places that יהוה cannot go?

We say that יהוה is everywhere; we also believe that God is one. Is there any contradiction between these two concepts?

To this day, many feel that the Western Wall, the remnant of the ancient Temple Mount, is a uniquely spiritual place. You can imagine, then, the anguish of the people when the Babylonians destroyed the Temple in 586 B.C.E. and sent the people of Israel into exile. It was in this historical context that the prophet Ezekiel appeared on the scene. Ezekiel had a vision of God that remains an enigma in the annals of our prophetic literature.

Ezekiel 1:1

וַיְהִי בִּשְׁלֹשִׁים שָׁנָה בָּרְבִיעִי בַּחֲמִשָּׁה לַחֹדֶשׁ וַאֲנִי בְתוֹךְ־
הַגּוֹלָה עַל־נְהַר כְּבָר נִפְתְּחוּ הַשָּׁמַיִם וָאֶרְאֶה מַרְאוֹת
אֱלֹהִים.

In the thirtieth year on the fifth day of the fourth month,
when I was in the community of exiles by the Chebar
Canal, the heavens opened and I saw visions of God.

Ezekiel 1:4–5

וָאֵרֶא וְהִנֵּה רוּחַ סְעָרָה בָּאָה מִן־הַצָּפוֹן עָנָן גָּדוֹל וְאֵשׁ
מִתְלַקַּחַת וְנֹגַהּ לוֹ סָבִיב וּמִתּוֹכָהּ כְּעֵין הַחַשְׁמַל מִתּוֹךְ
הָאֵשׁ: וּמִתּוֹכָהּ דְּמוּת אַרְבַּע חַיּוֹת וְזֶה מַרְאֵיהֶן דְּמוּת
אָדָם לָהֵנָּה.

I looked, and lo, a stormy wind came sweeping out of the
north—a huge cloud and flashing fire, surrounded by a
radiance; and in the center of it, in the center of the fire, a
gleam as of amber. In the center of it were also the figures
of four creatures. And this was their appearance: They had
the figures of human beings. However, each had four faces,
and each of them had four wings; the legs of each were a
single rigid leg, and the feet of each were like a single calf's
hoof, and their sparkle was like the luster of burnished
bronze.

Ezekiel 1:10–12

וּדְמוּת פְּנֵיהֶם פְּנֵי אָדָם וּפְנֵי אַרְיֵה אֶל־הַיָּמִין לְאַרְבַּעְתָּם
וּפְנֵי־שׁוֹר מֵהַשְּׂמֹאול לְאַרְבַּעְתָּן וּפְנֵי־נֶשֶׁר לְאַרְבַּעְתָּן:
וּפְנֵיהֶם וְכַנְפֵיהֶם פְּרֻדוֹת מִלְמָעְלָה לְאִישׁ שְׁתַּיִם חוֹבְרוֹת
אִישׁ וּשְׁתַּיִם מְכַסּוֹת אֵת גְּוִיֹּתֵיהֶנָה: וְאִישׁ אֶל־עֵבֶר פָּנָיו
יֵלֵכוּ אֶל אֲשֶׁר יִהְיֶה־שָּׁמָּה הָרוּחַ לָלֶכֶת יֵלֵכוּ לֹא יִסַּבּוּ
בְּלֶכְתָּן.

Each of them had a human face [at the front]; each of the
four had the face of a lion on the right; each of the four had
the face of an ox on the left; and each of the four had the
face of an eagle [at the back]. Such were their faces. As for
their wings, they were separated: above, each had two
touching those of the others, while the other two covered
its body. And each could move in the direction of any of its
faces; they went wherever the spirit impelled them to go,
without turning when they moved.

Ezekiel 1:15

וָאֵרֶא הַחַיּוֹת וְהִנֵּה אוֹפַן אֶחָד בָּאָרֶץ אֵצֶל הַחַיּוֹת
לְאַרְבַּעַת פָּנָיו.

As I gazed on the creatures, I saw one wheel on the ground
next to each of the four-faced creatures.

Ezekiel 1:19

וּבְלֶכֶת הַחַיּוֹת יֵלְכוּ הָאוֹפַנִּים אֶצְלָם וּבְהִנָּשֵׂא הַחַיּוֹת
מֵעַל הָאָרֶץ יִנָּשְׂאוּ הָאוֹפַנִּים.

And when the creatures moved forward, the wheels moved
at their sides; and when the creatures were borne above
the earth, the wheels were borne too.

Ezekiel 1:26

וּמִמַּעַל לָרָקִיעַ אֲשֶׁר עַל־רֹאשָׁם כְּמַרְאֵה אֶבֶן־סַפִּיר
דְּמוּת כִּסֵּא וְעַל דְּמוּת הַכִּסֵּא דְּמוּת כְּמַרְאֵה אָדָם עָלָיו
מִלְמָעְלָה:

Above the expanse over their heads was the semblance
of a throne, in appearance like sapphire; and on top, upon
this semblance of a throne, there was a semblance of a
human form.

Ezekiel 1:28

כְּמַרְאֵה הַקֶּשֶׁת אֲשֶׁר יִהְיֶה בֶעָנָן בְּיוֹם הַגֶּשֶׁם כֵּן מַרְאֵה
הַנֹּגַהּ סָבִיב הוּא מַרְאֵה דְּמוּת כְּבוֹד־יְהוָה וָאֶרְאֶה וָאֶפֹּל
עַל־פָּנַי וָאֶשְׁמַע קוֹל מְדַבֵּר.

Like the appearance of the rainbow that shines in the clouds on a rainy day, such was the appearance of the radiance that surrounded this semblance of the image of the Glory of *Adonai*. When I beheld it, I flung myself down on my face, and I heard the voice of someone speaking.

After all we have said about יהוה not having physical features or human attributes, Ezekiel's graphic depiction of God is startling. Does יהוה indeed have a face, and wings, and a "set of wheels"? As you might imagine, the image of Ezekiel's chariot has been the subject of much debate and inquiry throughout the ages. The mystics of the Kabbalah studied its mysteries as a way of elevating themselves spiritually through what was called *Merkavah* (chariot) mysticism. Some scholars have gone so far as to suggest that Ezekiel was taking hallucinogenic drugs; others have questioned his sanity.

How do you explain Ezekiel's vision of the chariot? Why might Ezekiel have envisioned יהוה in this way?

Ezekiel was living at a time when the people of Israel were being sent into exile. Their God was seen as dwelling in a specific place. The people of Israel, therefore, had both a religious and a political problem. With the Temple destroyed, what was to become of their faith—their relationship to יהוה?

Knowing this, why might Ezekiel have seen God as riding in a chariot?

Through his vision of the chariot, Ezekiel had made the God of the Israelites a portable God—a God who would come with them into exile and return with them later on.

In a way, Ezekiel's God was very much like our God—a God whom we take with us each and every day, a *Shechinah* who dwells with each and every one of us, no matter where we may travel, no matter how far we may stray.

My God Diary
Entry #13

Have you ever felt יהוה's presence in a remote place?
When and where?

Are there times when יהוה seems more distant? Why might this be? How might you answer the question of where יהוה was during the Inquisition, the Holocaust, the attack on the World Trade Center?

13. Theodicy: The Big Question

If God is all-powerful, all-knowing, and all-good, why do bad things keep happening to good people? This question is known as the problem of theodicy. Your answer to this question of theodicy will depend on the answers you have written so far in your God diary—on your own personal theology. The story of Noah, for instance, explains why bad things happen to people. In the story, the people weren't so good in the first place and therefore were punished. The Book of Lamentations, which was written after the destruction of the Temple in Jerusalem, also takes this perspective.

Lamentations 1:7

זָכְרָה יְרוּשָׁלַיִם יְמֵי עָנְיָהּ וּמְרוּדֶיהָ כֹּל מַחֲמֻדֶיהָ אֲשֶׁר הָיוּ
מִימֵי קֶדֶם בִּנְפֹל עַמָּהּ בְּיַד־צָר וְאֵין עוֹזֵר לָהּ רָאוּהָ צָרִים
שָׂחֲקוּ עַל־מִשְׁבַּתֶּהָ.

All the precious things she had in the days of old Jerusalem recalled in her days of woe and sorrow, when her people fell by enemy hands with none to help her; when enemies looked on and gloated over her downfall. Jerusalem has greatly sinned; therefore she has become a mockery.

Do we always bring about our own suffering, though? What about the innocent baby who is afflicted with a painful and fatal illness? How could it be that she deserves her fate?

In the Book of Job, we read that sometimes the innocent do suffer.

Job 1:6–21

וַיְהִי הַיּוֹם וַיָּבֹאוּ בְּנֵי הָאֱלֹהִים לְהִתְיַצֵּב עַל־יְהוָה וַיָּבוֹא
גַם־הַשָּׂטָן בְּתוֹכָם: וַיֹּאמֶר יְהוָה אֶל־הַשָּׂטָן מֵאַיִן תָּבֹא
וַיַּעַן הַשָּׂטָן אֶת־יְהוָה וַיֹּאמַר מִשּׁוּט בָּאָרֶץ וּמֵהִתְהַלֵּךְ בָּהּ:
וַיֹּאמֶר יְהוָה אֶל־הַשָּׂטָן הֲשַׂמְתָּ לִבְּךָ עַל־עַבְדִּי אִיּוֹב כִּי
אֵין כָּמֹהוּ בָּאָרֶץ אִישׁ תָּם וְיָשָׁר יְרֵא אֱלֹהִים וְסָר מֵרָע:
וַיַּעַן הַשָּׂטָן אֶת־יְהוָה וַיֹּאמַר הַחִנָּם יָרֵא אִיּוֹב אֱלֹהִים:
הֲלֹא־אַתָּ שַׂכְתָּ בַעֲדוֹ וּבְעַד־בֵּיתוֹ וּבְעַד כָּל־אֲשֶׁר־לוֹ
מִסָּבִיב מַעֲשֵׂה יָדָיו בֵּרַכְתָּ וּמִקְנֵהוּ פָּרַץ בָּאָרֶץ: וְאוּלָם
שְׁלַח־נָא יָדְךָ וְגַע בְּכָל־אֲשֶׁר־לוֹ אִם־לֹא עַל־פָּנֶיךָ יְבָרֲכֶךָּ:
וַיֹּאמֶר יְהוָה אֶל־הַשָּׂטָן הִנֵּה כָל־אֲשֶׁר־לוֹ בְּיָדֶךָ רַק אֵלָיו
אַל־תִּשְׁלַח יָדֶךָ וַיֵּצֵא הַשָּׂטָן מֵעִם פְּנֵי יְהוָה: וַיְהִי הַיּוֹם
וּבָנָיו וּבְנֹתָיו אֹכְלִים וְשֹׁתִים יַיִן בְּבֵית אֲחִיהֶם הַבְּכוֹר:
וּמַלְאָךְ בָּא אֶל־אִיּוֹב וַיֹּאמַר הַבָּקָר הָיוּ חֹרְשׁוֹת וְהָאֲתֹנוֹת
רֹעוֹת עַל־יְדֵיהֶם: וַתִּפֹּל שְׁבָא וַתִּקָּחֵם וְאֶת־הַנְּעָרִים הִכּוּ
לְפִי־חָרֶב וָאִמָּלְטָה רַק־אֲנִי לְבַדִּי לְהַגִּיד לָךְ: עוֹד זֶה
מְדַבֵּר וְזֶה בָּא וַיֹּאמַר אֵשׁ אֱלֹהִים נָפְלָה מִן־הַשָּׁמַיִם
וַתִּבְעַר בַּצֹּאן וּבַנְּעָרִים וַתֹּאכְלֵם וָאִמָּלְטָה רַק־אֲנִי לְבַדִּי
לְהַגִּיד לָךְ: עוֹד זֶה מְדַבֵּר וְזֶה בָּא וַיֹּאמַר כַּשְׂדִּים שָׂמוּ
שְׁלֹשָׁה רָאשִׁים וַיִּפְשְׁטוּ עַל־הַגְּמַלִּים וַיִּקָּחוּם וְאֶת־
הַנְּעָרִים הִכּוּ לְפִי־חָרֶב וָאִמָּלְטָה רַק־אֲנִי לְבַדִּי לְהַגִּיד
לָךְ: עַד זֶה מְדַבֵּר וְזֶה בָּא וַיֹּאמַר בָּנֶיךָ וּבְנוֹתֶיךָ אֹכְלִים
וְשֹׁתִים יַיִן בְּבֵית אֲחִיהֶם הַבְּכוֹר: וְהִנֵּה רוּחַ גְּדוֹלָה בָּאָה
מֵעֵבֶר הַמִּדְבָּר וַיִּגַּע בְּאַרְבַּע פִּנּוֹת הַבַּיִת וַיִּפֹּל עַל־הַנְּעָרִים
וַיָּמוּתוּ וָאִמָּלְטָה רַק־אֲנִי לְבַדִּי לְהַגִּיד לָךְ: וַיָּקָם אִיּוֹב
וַיִּקְרַע אֶת־מְעִלוֹ וַיָּגָז אֶת־רֹאשׁוֹ וַיִּפֹּל אַרְצָה וַיִּשְׁתָּחוּ:
וַיֹּאמֶר עָרֹם יָצָאתִי מִבֶּטֶן אִמִּי וְעָרֹם אָשׁוּב שָׁמָּה יְהוָה
נָתַן וַיהוָה לָקָח יְהִי שֵׁם יְהוָה מְבֹרָךְ.

One day the angels presented themselves before *Adonai*, and Satan came along with them. *Adonai* said to Satan, "Where have you been?" Satan answered *Adonai*, "I have been roaming all over the earth." *Adonai* said to Satan, "Have you noticed My servant Job? There is no one like him on earth, a blameless and upright man who fears God and shuns evil." Satan answered *Adonai*, "Does Job not have good reason to fear God? Why, it is You who have fenced him round, him and his household and all that he has. You have blessed his efforts so that his possessions spread out in the land. But lay Your hand upon all that he has and he will surely curse You to Your face. *Adonai* replied to Satan, "See, all that he has is in your power; only do not lay a hand on him." Satan departed from the presence of *Adonai*.

One day as his sons and daughters were eating and drinking wine in the house of their eldest brother, a messenger came to Job and said, "The oxen were plowing and the donkeys were grazing alongside them when Sabeans attacked them and carried them off, and put the boys to the sword; I alone have escaped to tell you." This one was still speaking when another came and said, "God's fire fell from heaven, took hold of the sheep and the boys, and burned them up; I alone have escaped to tell you." This one was still speaking when another came and said, "A Chaldean formation of three columns made a raid on the camels and carried them off and put the boys to the sword; I alone have escaped to tell you." This one was still speaking when another came and said, "Your sons and daughters were eating and drinking wine in the house of their eldest brother when suddenly a mighty wind came from the wilderness. It struck the four corners of the house so that it collapsed upon the young people and they died; I alone have escaped to tell you."

Then Job arose, tore his robe, cut off his hair, and threw himself on the ground and worshiped. He said, "Naked came I out of my mother's womb, and naked shall I return there; *Adonai* has given, *Adonai* has taken away, blessed be the name of *Adonai*."

In both of these biblical texts, life is depicted as a game of chess, with God (and here also Satan) as the great Chess Master in the heavens, directing our lives for good or for bad like pawns on a chessboard. If bad things happen to good people, therefore, there must be a reason. In the story of Noah, and in the Book of Lamentations, the reason for suffering is that we have sinned. In the story of Job, there is also a reason, though it is beyond human understanding. Perhaps something good will arise out of the evil that has befallen us, or perhaps יהוה has reasons that we simply cannot comprehend.

But what if life is not like a game of chess, but rather a game of backgammon? In backgammon the players throw dice to determine their moves. The roll of the dice is random, but the play thereafter is based on skill. A better player will win more often, but not always. A terrible player may get such extraordinary rolls that she cannot help but win. In other words, there may be randomness in the universe. יהוה may be more present in our response to the rolls that we receive than in the rolls themselves. Illness, therefore, may be caused by a random combination of genetic and environmental factors. For strength in dealing with the challenge of illness, however, we are able to turn to יהוה, as expressed here in this beautiful meditation from *Gates of Prayer*.

Gates of Prayer (1994); page 75

Prayer invites God to let the Divine Presence suffuse our spirits, to let the Divine will prevail in our lives. Prayer cannot bring water to parched fields, nor mend a broken bridge, nor rebuild a ruined city; but prayer can water an arid soul, mend a broken heart, and rebuild a weakened will.

Gates of Prayer (New York: CCAR, 1994)

Do you agree with this meditation? Can God bring water to parched fields, mend a broken bridge, or rebuild a ruined city? If so, how?

Of course, if God is indeed everywhere, how can there be randomness in the world? One answer may be found in the theology of Isaac Luria that we explored in chapter 10.

If יהוה contracted in order to create a vacuum and leave space for the universe, how might this explain the existence of evil in the world?

Luria also believed that we have the potential to repair the world. This process he calls *tikkun olam*. Every time we perform a mitzvah (commandment), it is as if we are collecting a spark of God and putting the shards of our broken world back together. Through the process of *tikkun olam* we can heal the world and bring about a perfect day, which Jews call the Messianic Age.

My God Diary
Entry #14

Why do bad things happen to good people? How does your image of יהוה affect your answer to this question of theodicy? Do you feel that יהוה controls everything that happens, or is there randomness in the universe?

Can you think of anyone who has received terrible "rolls of the dice" in life, but who nevertheless has managed to build a magnificent life? Do you know of anyone who has received wonderful "rolls of the dice," but whose life has nonetheless been misspent?

14. The Final Chapter

Just as Buber and Maimonides understood God in different ways; just as Moses' vision of God was so very different from that of Ezekiel, so each of us has our own understanding of the Eternal God.

The prayer known as the *Avot V'Imahot* begins with the following words:

בָּרוּךְ אַתָּה יְיָ, אֱלֹהֵינוּ וֵאלֹהֵי אֲבוֹתֵינוּ וְאִמּוֹתֵינוּ: אֱלֹהֵי אַבְרָהָם, אֱלֹהֵי יִצְחָק, וֵאלֹהֵי יַעֲקֹב. אֱלֹהֵי שָׂרָה, אֱלֹהֵי רִבְקָה, אֱלֹהֵי לֵאָה, וֵאלֹהֵי רָחֵל.

Blessed are You, *Adonai*, our God and God of our ancestors, God of Abraham, God of Isaac, and God of Jacob, God of Sarah, God of Rebekah, God of Leah, and God of Rachel.

Why, our Rabbis ask, does the prayer not say, "God of Abraham, Isaac, and Jacob," rather than mentioning "God of..." repeatedly?

The answer they offer is that this shows that Abraham's vision of God differed from that of Isaac, as Sarah's vision of God differed from that of Rachel. Each of our ancestors had his or her own vision of and relationship with God.

This point is underscored in the following midrash.

B'midbar Rabbah 21:2

וידבר משה אל ה' יפקוד ה' וגו' הלכה אם ראה הרבה אוכלוסין של בני אדם אומר בא"י אלהינו מלך העולם חכם הרזים כשם שאין פרצופותיהן דומין זה לזה כך

אין דעתן שוין זה לזה אלא כל אחד ואחד יש לו דעה
בפני עצמו וכה"א (איוב כח) לעשות לרוח משקל
לרוחות של כל בריה ובריה תדע לך שהוא כן שכן
משה מבקש מן הקב"ה בשעת מיתה אמר לפניו רבש"ע
גלוי וידוע לפניך דעתן של כל אחד ואחד ואין דעתן של
בניך דומין זה לזה וכשאני מסתלק מהן בבקשה ממך
מנה עליהם מנהיג שיהא סובלם לאחד ואחד לפי דעתו
שנאמר יפקד ה' הרוח אינו אומר אלא הרוחות.

MOSES SPOKE TO ADONAI, SAYING, LET ADONAI, THE SPIRITS OF
ALL FLESH, APPOINT A MAN OVER THE CONGREGATION.
(Numbers 27:15)

If one sees a great multitude of people s/he should say:
"Blessed are You, Adonai, our God, Ruler of the universe,
who knows their innermost secrets." For, as their faces are
not like each other, so are their temperaments dissimilar as
well, each individual having a personality of his or her own.
In this vein it is written, GOD WEIGHS THE SPIRITS (WINDS)
(Job 28:25). This indicates that God does so for the spirit of
each individual human being. The proof of this can be found
in the request that Moses made of the Holy One, blessed
be God, in the hour of his death. Moses said to God
"Sovereign of the universe, the mind of every individual is
revealed and known to You, yet the minds of Your children
are not similar to one another. Now that I am leaving them,
please appoint over them a leader who will deal with each
one of them as his or her temperament requires." This may
be inferred from the verse, LET ADONAI, THE SPIRITS OF ALL
FLESH, APPOINT A MAN OVER THE CONGREGATION.... It does
not say the spirit but rather, "THE SPIRITS."

The use of the plural here implies that God relates to all of the spirits, each according to its own needs and idiosyncrasies.

How might an individual's personality or life experience affect his or her vision of the One God?

And so we come back to the elephant. God is a King and a Mothering Presence, a Rock and a Chariot, a Shepherd and the Wind of the Universe, an Eternal Thou and the Prime Mover, a God on High and the Still Small Voice within us, and so much more. Each of us perceives יהוה and must seek to express יהוה's nature in his or her own way. That is why the "My God Diary" sections represent the most important pages in this book. Go back and read your diary entries now.

In this book we have explored only a few of the myriad ways in which Jewish souls have understood יהוה. Now it is your turn.

My God Diary
Entry #15

Write about your own concepts of, and feelings for, יהוה.

How have your God ideas changed since your first diary entry?

111

Afterword

My God Diary: Author's Entry

I was a teenage atheist.

Until one day when, as a sophomore at Princeton University, I became engaged in a philosophical debate with my roommate, Bill. I, the rabbi's son, argued that the world was nothing but a chance combination of physical principles and preexisting matter. He, the engineer, agreed that the world was certainly all of that, but asserted that there was also "something more." The debate raged on into the wee hours of the morning, as such discussions tend to do in college. Before long we were simply going back and forth saying, "Something More," "Nothing But," "Something More," "Nothing But." Finally, I decided to break the deadlock. I posed the following scenario:

"Bill," I said, "imagine that you are a scientist in the year 8765. You and your colleagues now know everything there is to know about biology, chemistry, and physics, and you have just invented a machine that can put molecules together in any formation that you desire. So you pour the component parts of a human body into the machine: hydrogen and oxygen, carbon and calcium, a bit of zinc, and some manganese. You now program the machine to rearrange the molecules into the form of a human baby."

I could almost taste victory on my lips as I spoke. "Now, would the resultant being be a fully formed human soul that would wet its diaper, grow, learn, and come to love its mother, or would it be a blob that would look a lot like a human baby?" I looked up with a triumphant smile. Then I began to frown. I realized that I believed it would be a blob, that it would need "something more" to become a fully formed human being—a soul, if you will, a *n'shamah*, a breath of God. And my life was changed.

I did not go out the next day and develop a relationship with יהוה; that took some time. But the crack that had been made in my shell of skepticism was just enough to let some feelings in. So that when I stood at the Western Wall in Jerusalem, beneath the *chuppah* with my bride, in the birthing rooms of my children, the feeling of יהוה was able to enter, and I was able to come to know God as an Eternal Thou.

In chapter 6, I asked you to create your own names for God. My personal name for יהוה is "The Something More of the Universe," for it was the intellectual understanding that the world is "something more" that has allowed me to feel יהוה in my life.

In my experience, there are no atheists in birthing rooms. Holding your child in your arms for the first time, you simply know that he or she is something more than a chance combination of chemicals and physical principles. So it is not surprising that my theology was transformed again when the life of my firstborn child, Ariella, was threatened. She was seven years old when we allowed her to travel to northern Michigan with friends. Ariella, her friend Molly, and Molly's mother were eating lunch in a restaurant. Suddenly, without warning, a tornado tore through the building. One half of the diner was completely destroyed. Our friend had gotten the girls under a table and—thankfully—no one was hurt. When I received the news, I *benched gomeil*—I said a prayer thanking God for saving my daughter. Theologically, however, I had to make a choice. If I was going to give God credit for saving my daughter, I would also have to blame God if she had been sitting on the other side of the restaurant and perished. I simply did not believe, I realized then, that my God would throw tornadoes at little girls.

Of course, this begs the question. Why should we pray? Personally, I have prayed for a new Jaguar to appear in my driveway, and somehow it has not happened. God is not a great candy machine in the sky into which you put prayer tokens in order to receive bars of happiness. But when I pray for courage, God grants me courage. When I pray for perspective, I gain perspective. When I pray for inner peace, I somehow feel more peaceful. And sometimes when I ask for nothing at all, I am blessed simply with a few moments spent in the presence of יהוה, basking in God's Eternal light. It is not just an act of meditation for me; it is something more. As is the world, as are we all.

Notes

[1] Edwin Abbott, *Flatland: A Romance of Many Dimensions* (Great Britain: Seely & Co., 1884).

[2] "A Talk with Einstein," *The Listener,* September 1955.

[3] In *The Hand of God: Thoughts and Images Reflecting the Spirit of the Universe,* ed. Michael Reagan (Philadelphia and London: Templeton Foundation Press, 1999), 32.

[4] *Science and Religion,* 1940, New York. "Einstein: His Life and Times" by Phillip Frank, page 286.

[5] Address at the Princeton Theological Seminary.